More adventures
of Robin Hood

John Turvey

Longman

500 word
vocabulary

Longman Group Limited,
Longman House, Burnt Mill, Harlow,
Essex CM20 2JE, England
Associated Companies throughout the world.

Fifth impression 1986

ISBN 0 582 52656 6

Produced by Longman Group (FE) Ltd
Printed in Hong Kong

Acknowledgements

We are grateful to the BBC for permission to reproduce copyright material. We are also grateful to the following: Miles Anderson for opposite page I; Tony Steedman for pages 17 (right) and 53; Paul Darrow for page 17 (left); Richard Speight (left,), Bernard Archard (centre) and Stephen Whittaker (second right) for page 30; Kevin Storey for page 34; Martin Potter for the frontispiece and pages 30 (right), 40, 43, 50 (left), and the cover; Diane Keen for page 40 and the cover; Conrad Asquith for pages 30 (second left) and 50 (centre); Anthony Counter for page 50 (right).

Contents

page

Words outside Stage 1 of the New Method Supplementary Readers are in a list on pages 56 and 57.

Note

Was there once a man called Robin Hood? Some people think so, and others think not. But there are many old stories about him.

When bad men took his lands, he ran away to Sherwood Forest near Nottingham. There he lived with his friends: Little John, Friar Tuck and many others. They killed and ate the king's deer, and stole from the rich.

King Richard, who ruled then, was always fighting in other countries. So his brother, John, ruled England for him. Prince John was a bad man, and his sheriff in Nottingham was no better.

The Sheriff was always trying to catch Robin Hood and kill him. But Robin Hood knew the forest well, and the people loved him. He was not afraid of the Sheriff and his men.

The story of Reynold Greenleaf

The place – Nottingham. The time – one sunny September afternoon, a year after Robin Hood went into the forest. It was good to be alive on a day like that. But the Sheriff did not look happy as he rode out of the city. He stopped to look at some men near the walls. They were shooting with bows and arrows. They were all good, but best of all was a big man with a beard. His shot was the best every time.

"I have work for that man. Tell him to come here," he said to one of his men.

The last few weeks had been a bad time for the Sheriff. There were thieves in Sherwood Forest. Rich men had lost their money there. Even the Sheriff did not like to go through it without many soldiers. "If I have a man like that with me," he thought, "I'll never be afraid of anybody in the forest."

When the man came up, the Sheriff looked at him. He saw that he was not just big; he was a giant. "What's your name, and whose man are you?" he asked.

"Reynold Greenleaf," answered the giant, "and

I'm nobody's man but my own. If you want, I'll be yours."

"That is just what I *do* want," said the Sheriff. "Come to the castle tomorrow. My men will tell you what to do."

At the castle
So Reynold Greenleaf became one of the Sheriff's men. Everywhere the Sheriff went, he went, too. He stood by his chair at dinner. He rode with him in the forest. Soon Reynold Greenleaf knew everything about the Sheriff – where he went, what he did, who he saw. Even the place in his bedroom where he put his money.

Nobody in the castle liked the Sheriff. He was always angry, always shouting, always calling people names. It was always "Come here, Frog-face," or "Answer me, Wooden-head." When he was not there his men called him names, too – but not Reynold Greenleaf. He never said anything bad about the Sheriff. Because of this the others did not like him.

"He runs after the Sheriff like a dog," they said. But Reynold Greenleaf never said anything.

When the Sheriff saw this, he was glad. "Reynold Greenleaf is a good man," he thought. "He is not like the others, who call me bad names. When he came to work for me, the forest thieves were stealing money every week. Now it has all stopped.

When Reynold Greenleaf rides with me, that
Robin Hood is afraid to show his face."

Reynold Greenleaf is ill

December, January and February went by. Still
nobody had seen Robin Hood and his men. Some
said they had moved out of the forest. Others said
Robin Hood had gone over the sea.

Then, one day in March, the Sheriff got up and
said: "Today I shall go into the forest. I want to
look at the king's deer. Prince John may come this
way soon. He will be angry if he finds no deer.
I will see what I can catch today."

So he sent a note to his men in the forest. He told
them to have dogs and horses ready. Then, when
he had eaten, he called for Reynold Greenleaf. But
nobody could find him.

"Where *is* the man?" shouted the Sheriff angrily.
"I must have him with me today!"

Then somebody said: "He's still in bed. He says
he's ill – too ill to sit on a horse."

"Ill?" cried the Sheriff. "I don't pay men to be ill!
Tell him this. I'm going to the forest now. If he
doesn't get up and ride after me, he'll lose a day's
pay!"

With that, he got on to his horse and rode out of
the castle with his men.

Reynold Greenleaf looks for food

Reynold Greenleaf was in bed in the castle. He

heard the noise of the Sheriff and his men as they went. He laughed. He did not look at all ill. He jumped out of bed and dressed. Then he went down to the great hall. The Sheriff's men got their food and drink there. But the man who gave it out was just shutting it up.

"Sheriff's dog!" the man said, "you're too late. There's no more food. And if you don't like it, you can tell the Sheriff himself."

Reynold Greenleaf did not say a word. He took the man in his hands and threw him across the hall. The man hit the floor hard and stayed there, not moving.

Reynold Greenleaf then looked for some food. But he did not like what he found. So he went down to the place where they cooked the food. The cook was not there, so he sat down by the fire. Something in a pot was cooking there, and he took some.

"This is good," he said, as he began to eat.

Reynold meets the cook
He had not eaten much before the cook walked in with some eggs. When he saw Reynold Greenleaf, the eggs nearly fell from his hands. "Well!" he said, Do you know that you are eating the Sheriff's dinner?"

He put the eggs down. He was a short man, but he had long arms, and a body like iron. He walked across to Reynold Greenleaf and hit him so hard that he fell off his chair. The pot broke, and the Sheriff's dinner went all over the stone floor.

"You're a little man, but you hit hard," said Reynold Greenleaf as he got up. He took out his sword. "Show me if you can hit as hard with a sword."

"Little man!" cried the cook angrily. "I *will* show you." He went out and came back with another sword.

"It's a long sword for a short man," said Reynold Greenleaf, laughing. "Try not to fall over it."

The fight

They began to fight. Clang! Clash! The noise of their swords rang round the room. But when at last they stopped, there was not the smallest cut on Reynold or the cook.

"You fight well, little Cook," said Reynold Greenleaf. "Give me your hand. Come with me to the forest. I will find you a better man to cook for. I can show you how to shoot with a bow, too."

"A bow? I'm happier with a sword in my hand. But I would like to cook for another man," answered the cook. "Nothing is ever as this Sheriff wants it. It is always 'This is too hot', or 'That is too cold' or 'You've cooked this too much.' I think I will go with you."

"Good!" said Reynold Greenleaf. "But before

we go, come with me to the Sheriff's room.
Remember, we must take our pay. Then – off to
the forest. There, you will cook one last dinner for
him. And you must make it a good one. He will
pay for it – more than he has ever paid for any
dinner in all his life."

Reynold Greenleaf in the forest
The Sheriff had had a bad day. He did not catch
any deer. He lost his dogs, and he fell off his horse
into some water. But one thing made him glad.
He had not seen Robin Hood and his men. "He's
afraid of us," he said to Baldwin, the man who
helped him with his work. "He has gone away.
Now I can ride where I like. I can do without that
lazy, good-for-nothing Reynold Greenleaf."

"But if Robin Hood has gone away from the
forest, why are there so few deer?" asked Baldwin.

The Sheriff could not think of an answer. So he
was glad when he saw a man on a horse coming
towards him. It was Reynold Greenleaf.

"Humph!" said the Sheriff. "Why do you come
at this time? It is all over now. You can ride back
to Nottingham again. Just tell that cook of mine
that I am coming. I want my dinner as soon as I get
in."

"Sheriff," said Reynold Greenleaf, "don't go
back so soon. I don't know how many deer you
have killed today—"

"Humph!" said the Sheriff again, angrily.

"—but I have just seen the biggest deer in the forest. I saw it as I was coming to find you. You must see it before it moves away. And if you like, I will shoot it with my bow."

The Sheriff thought: "The day will soon be over, and I want to get back to Nottingham. But I haven't even caught a rabbit. My men will laugh if I go back with nothing."

"Wait here for the dogs to come up," he said at last to Baldwin. And then to Reynold Greenleaf: "Lead on. But if there is no giant deer, you will no longer work for the Sheriff of Nottingham."

Who shoots the king's deer?

Reynold Greenleaf rode quickly. The Sheriff was fat and found it hard to stay near him. But, at last, they came to a small open place. There they found the deer. It was very big, as Reynold Greenleaf had said. But it was on the ground with an arrow in its side. Dead.

The Sheriff got down from his horse. "Who has done this?" he shouted angrily. "Who shoots the king's deer in my forest?"

"I," said a man, whom he had not seen in the dying afternoon light. His green clothes made him hard to see in any light. "But it's not *your* forest. It's *mine*."

"We'll see about that," said the Sheriff. "Reynold

Greenleaf, take this man to Nottingham. Tomorrow he shall die!"

"Sheriff," said Reynold Greenleaf, "in the forest I do not answer to that name. Here, they call me Little John."

"Little John!" cried the Sheriff. He knew that name. For a time he could say no more. There was nothing to say. "Have I had one of Robin Hood's men in my castle for so long?" he thought. "And you...you..." he said at last, looking at the man in green, "...you must be Robin Hood. Oh! I have done a foolish thing!"

Robin Hood takes the Sheriff

More men in green came from the trees. They put the dead deer on the Sheriff's horse. Then they all walked off into the forest, taking the Sheriff with them. Far away, the Sheriff's men were blowing their horns. They were trying to find where he had gone. But their noise became harder and harder to hear. Soon the Sheriff could hear nothing but the trees.

At last, they got to the place where Robin Hood and his men lived.

"The Sheriff won't be with us for long," said Robin Hood to his men. "We must make him happy. Bring food and drink."

Robin Hood's words made the Sheriff afraid. "I don't like those words *won't be with us for long*," he thought. "What's he going to do with me?"

Dinner in the forest
They sat down to dinner by a big fire. The Sheriff
was still afraid, but he wanted to eat, too. He had
had a hard day.

"Fill a glass for the Sheriff," cried Robin Hood.
A beautiful glass was put into his hand. The
Sheriff's face went white. It was one of his own
glasses – the ones he loved so much. But he said
nothing.

"Bring food for the Sheriff," said Robin Hood.
They brought food, and it was very good.

"Your cook is as good as mine," he said.

"My cook is the same as yours," Robin Hood
answered. "Come to the table, Cook. The Sheriff
wants to thank you."

The Sheriff's face went even whiter when he saw
his own cook. "You, too?" he said.

After they had eaten, they all slept round the
fire – Robin Hood's men making a ring round the
Sheriff. The Sheriff had not tried to sleep on the
ground before. It was hard, and he was awake all
night looking at the stars.

The next morning
Morning came at last. Robin Hood's men washed
in cold water. But the Sheriff did not like cold
water in a cold forest. Then they sat down at the

table, and again they ate and drank.

"Well, Sheriff," said Robin Hood. "I am a kind man. I think I shall not kill you today. Or tomorrow. Or even the day after that—"

The Sheriff began to look happier.

"—*if*—" Robin Hood had more to say. "*If* we can live in the forest as we want. *If* you and your soldiers stop trying to catch us. If not – you must stay with us in the forest."

The Sheriff thought of the cold water in the morning. He thought of the hard stones under his back at night. "Never!" he said. "You can live in this forest for as long as you like. I want to get back to my castle."

"Then you can go," said Robin Hood, as he helped the Sheriff on to his horse, "when you have paid Reynold Greenleaf for his work."

"But I can't pay him here," answered the Sheriff. "I haven't any money."

"Oh, but you have. Bring me the Sheriff's moneybags." One of Robin Hood's men went off and came back with some bags. The Sheriff thought that these bags were in his bedroom. But Little John and Cook had brought them with them. It was the unhappiest part of the Sheriff's short stay with Robin Hood. His face looked ten years older as Robin Hood put his hand into one of the bags. He took out some money and gave it to Little John.

"That's too much," said Little John. "On the last

day I stayed in bed. The Sheriff said he would not pay me for that day."

"Well," said Robin Hood, "we must pay the Sheriff back one day's pay." He gave a little money back to the Sheriff. "Take that. The other money we shall give to the poor."

Then they led the Sheriff out of the forest. He rode back to Nottingham with a little money and a lot to think about.

Robin Hood and the fishermen

On sunny days it was good to live in the forest. But after September, the days grew shorter. The air grew colder. The rain came down every day. The forest was not a good place to live in then.

So about this time, Robin Hood and his men sometimes went on journeys. They looked for a friendly house in a place where nobody asked any questions. And there they lived, waiting for March or April.

Robin Hood sometimes went to a little place near the sea. A few fishermen lived there. They did not know who he was. But the old woman he stayed with knew. Her man had died many years before, and her sons had gone away. All she had was a boat. Some of the fishermen went fishing in it, and gave her half their fish.

When Robin Hood had stayed with her before, she had been a happy old woman. But this time he could see at once that she had changed.

"What is it, Mother Margery?" he asked one day. "Why do you go about with a sad face? You get money from me, and money from your fish. You live well."

"Ah, Robin Hood," she said, "I don't live as well as you think. I do not get much fish from my boat.

The fishermen bring back fish, and they give me some. But do they show me all the fish they have caught? I don't know. I think they may hide some."

"If you think that," said Robin Hood, "send me out with them in the boat. I will see what they do."

Robin Hood meets Blackbeard

So next morning, Robin Hood took his bow (he took it everywhere), and went down to the sea. There he found four fishermen getting the boat ready.

"Good morning, friends," he said. "Mother Margery has sent me to help you. She says I never do any work. So here I am. You must tell me how to catch fish."

"I'll tell you one thing now . . ." said the biggest of the four. He was a man with a long, black beard. "We don't catch fish with a bow and arrow." The others laughed.

"Who knows what I may catch?" answered Robin Hood. And he got into the boat.

Blackbeard told the others to put the sail up, and the boat moved quickly out to sea. They had not gone far before Robin Hood began to be ill. The sea was not at all like the forest. The boat went up and down . . . up and down . . . up and down. And his face became as green as his own clothes. When the fishermen put out their nets, he could not do anything. He just lay down and shut his eyes.

Long Jankin

The day went by, and he began to get a little better. At last, he stood up and helped them take in their nets. It was hard work.

"You see what fishing is like," said Blackbeard. "It is not like waiting in a forest for the trees to grow." He laughed.

Robin Hood said nothing. He was looking at a bigger boat that was coming quickly towards them. "What is that boat?" he said at last.

"God help us!" cried Blackbeard. "It's Long Jankin and his men. Quick! Quick! Put up the sail."

The others put up the sail, and the boat moved back towards the land. But the other boat came after them.

"Who is this Long Jankin?" asked Robin Hood.

"He comes from across the sea," said one of the fishermen. "He steals what he can get from other boats. He will take our catch of fish if he gets us. Look! You can see him now."

Robin Hood looked. The other boat was getting nearer, and he could see a big red-faced man with a sword in his hand. There were other ugly-looking men with swords and knives, too.

Robin Hood put an arrow in his bow. He had never tried to shoot from a boat before. Up and down went Mother Margery's boat. Up and down went the sea. Up and down went Long Jankin's boat. He had thought of a way to save them. But how could he shoot when everything was moving?

He sent off one arrow, and it went through Long Jankin's sail. The next one did not hit anything at all. This was not a good place to shoot from. He could not even stand up.

"Sit round me," he said to the fishermen. "Put your hands on me to stop me falling, and I will save you."

They all sat down and did what he said. He could stand up without falling now. But the other boat was very near. And Long Jankin's men were getting ready to jump.

Robin Hood shot again. This time he did what he wanted to do. The arrow cut through the rope that made the sail stay up. The sail fell down. The wooden arm along the top of it hit Long Jankin's head, and he fell into the sea. Without its sail the boat soon stopped moving. But Mother Margery's boat went on towards the land. They were saved.

Mother Margery gets more fish
From that day, Blackbeard changed. He did not laugh at Robin Hood as he did before. Robin Hood never found out if Blackbeard and his men took too much of the old woman's fish. But from that day, old Mother Margery *did* get more fish. Why? Were the fishermen afraid of Robin Hood? Was it because Long Jankin never stole from them again? Or were there just more fish? We shall never know.

Set a thief to catch a thief

The Sheriff's face was white as he sat at dinner in his hall. He was very angry. He took his glass in his hand and threw it across the room.

"Another one today," he said. "A rich man from London lost £500. Then he came to me and said: 'Why don't you go out and catch these thieves? I shall tell Prince John when I get to London.'"

"Was it Robin Hood again?" asked Baldwin. He was a quick little man with a face like a fox.

"Who do you think it was?" shouted the Sheriff. "Yes, it was Robin Hood." He put out his hand for another thing to throw. This time it was Baldwin's dinner. "What can we do? We lead our soldiers into the forest, and we find nobody. We lead them out of the forest again, and Robin Hood comes back."

"We must think harder," said Baldwin. "Remember what people say: set a thief to catch a thief. We don't know how Robin Hood thinks. We don't know where he hides. We don't know how he moves about. Another thief would know all this. Remember, we caught one last week. If

we don't kill him, he may help us to catch Robin
Hood. Guy of Gisborne could be the man for work
like this."

The Sheriff sat there without saying anything.
He bit the legs off a duck and began eating them.
He was thinking. At last he rubbed his hands over
his beard to clean them, and said: "Bring Guy of
Gisborne to me."

Guy of Gisborne

Now Robin Hood, as you know, was a thief. But
he was not a thief like Guy of Gisborne. Robin
Hood took money from the rich and gave it to the
poor. Even when he stole from the rich he sometimes asked them to have dinner with him. And

he was always kind to women and children. He killed to save himself or his men, but not to steal.

But Guy of Gisborne was a hard man. He killed like a beast, because he liked killing. He had no friends, and rode about the forest alone. Over his head and body he wore a horse's skin. He looked just like a horse riding another horse. He did this to make people afraid of him. And they were.

Everybody was glad when the Sheriff caught him. "Now the Sheriff will kill him," they thought. But a few weeks after that, Guy was back in the forest again. Why did the Sheriff open the castle gate for him?

The letter

Robin Hood and Little John were sitting under a big tree beside a forest road. Sometimes they spoke, but mostly they sat there listening. They were waiting for someone to come along the road.

"I don't like it," said Little John. "You get this letter shot by a bow—

MEET ME AT THE BIG TREE WHERE THE TWO ROADS MEET.
I WILL SHOW YOU WHO IS THE BETTER MAN WITH A SWORD.

Who sent it? If it is not some fool playing a game, it may be the Sheriff. I think he is trying to catch you."

"Don't be afraid of the Sheriff," said Robin Hood. "He's more afraid of us. No, I think the man who wrote this letter wants to become one of us. There's always a place here for a man who can fight well."

"Afraid!" said Little John angrily. "You know I'm not afraid of the Sheriff or anyone. But it isn't brave to do foolish things like this."

"Oh!" said Robin Hood. "Foolish am I? If you think—"

Before they had time to quarrel more, they heard a noise. A horse and rider were coming through the forest. But who, or what was it? Was it a man on a horse, or a horse on a horse? As he came nearer they could see it was a man. A man, yes – but dressed in a horseskin!

"Little John," said Robin Hood, "go back to the others now. I know who this is. I've wanted to meet him for a long time, and I must meet him alone."

Robin Hood meets Guy of Gisborne
Little John was still angry, but he went off through the trees without a word. Robin Hood stayed there, sitting with his back to the tree.

"What can I do for you?" he asked, as the man

under the skin stopped in front of him.

"You can show me where I can find Robin Hood."

"I can do that. But I must tell you something. Robin Hood doesn't like men who are afraid to show their faces."

The man jumped off his horse and threw his horseskin on to the ground. He had brown, wolf-like teeth, and eyes that moved about all the time. He walked towards Robin Hood with his sword in his hand. "Take me to Robin Hood," he shouted, "or I'll cut you into little bits."

Unafraid, Robin Hood stood up and looked at him. "And he does not like men who shout," he said, putting his hand round the other side of the tree. He had put his sword there, where nobody could see it. "Lastly," he said, with his sword in his hand, "Robin Hood does not like a thief dressed like a donkey, Guy of Gisborne."

The fight

They fought. Guy of Gisborne was bigger. But Robin Hood was quick on his feet, and they fought for a long time. Robin Hood gave Guy of Gisborne some bad cuts across the face. But at last Guy hit Robin's sword so hard that it fell out of his hand.

"I think only Robin Hood could fight so long with me," said Guy. "But whoever you are, you have fought your last fight."

He ran at Robin Hood to kill him. But the horse-skin caught his feet, and he fell. At once Robin Hood jumped on him. He took the sword from his hand, and drove it through his body. Guy of Gisborne was dead.

Robin Hood becomes Guy of Gisborne

Robin Hood sat down under the big tree again. He began to think. Not about the body which was growing cold in front of him, but about Little John. "I'll give him something to think about," he said to himself.

He looked at Guy of Gisborne's face. It had got badly cut in the fight. Few people would know who he was now. Without his clothes nobody would know him. "If I changed clothes with him," thought Robin Hood, "what would people think then?"

He changed clothes very quickly. Then he blew his horn three times, and put the horseskin over his own head.

"Now Little John will think I am Guy of Gisborne, and that the dead man is me," he said.

From far off came the noise of an answering horn, and not long after, he heard men running through the forest. He laughed under his horseskin. Then men began to come through the trees, and at once he stopped laughing. What was happening? These were not his men. They were the Sheriff's!

Little John is caught

After Little John had left Robin Hood, he had walked back towards the others. As he got nearer, he began to hear shouts and the noise of sword on sword. He started to run.

"God save us!" he cried when he saw what was happening. The Sheriff's men were there. The huts where they lived were on fire. One or two of Robin Hood's men were dead on the ground. Others were running off into the forest.

Guy of Gisborne had done his work well. He had found where they all lived, and had brought the Sheriff and his men there. His letter, too, had led Robin Hood and Little John away from their men. Without them, their men did not know what to do.

Little John did not know all this then. But he knew that he must try to save his friends. The Sheriff's men had now seen him, and they had stopped. They remembered him as Reynold Greenleaf and were afraid of him. He put an arrow in his bow. But just as he was getting ready to shoot, his bow broke. "Oh, why must this happen now?" he thought. He put his hand on his sword. But before he could take it out, the Sheriff's men had jumped on him. He fought them. He kicked them. He bit them. No one could fight better than Little John. But there were too many of them. At last they tied him across a horse, ready to take back to Nottingham.

"I'll kill Little John"

Now we must go back to Robin Hood. In the beginning, when he had seen the Sheriff's men all round him, he was afraid. But when the Sheriff spoke, he soon remembered that nobody knew that he was Robin Hood. The horseskin covered his face.

"You've done well, Guy of Gisborne," the Sheriff said. He looked at the body on the ground, and rubbed his hands happily. "You've killed Robin Hood. We've caught the one they call Little John."

"What will you do with this Little John?" asked Robin Hood. When he spoke under the horseskin it was just like Guy of Gisborne speaking.

"Kill him," answered the Sheriff. "He'll die on the city walls tomorrow, and I'll put his head on the gates. Everyone will see what happens to deer thieves."

"Why must you take him back to Nottingham?" asked Robin Hood. "I've killed Robin Hood here in the forest. I'll kill Little John here, too. He has friends everywhere, even in Nottingham. It's better to kill him quickly before they hear that we've caught him."

"This Guy of Gisborne kills well," said Baldwin. "See what he did to Robin Hood. Even his Maid Marion wouldn't know him now!"

The Sheriff thought about it. He had caught

Little John, and he did not want to lose him. As long as he stayed alive he had time to get away. Robin Hood's men were all too good at getting away.

"Do it, then," he said. "We can still take his head back to Nottingham."

Robin Hood and Little John get away
When they got back to Little John and the others, Robin Hood said: "Stand away from the horse." He made the Sheriff's men move back. Now the horse with Little John on its back was standing by itself. Robin Hood got on to another horse and took his sword out.

"This is how I'll kill him. I'll ride up to the horse quickly, and as I go by, I'll make one cut with my sword. Little John's head will fall to the ground."

Before the Sheriff could say yes or no, Robin Hood began to ride towards Little John. But when he came up to Little John's horse, he hit it hard with the side of his sword. The horse was afraid. It began to run after Robin Hood's horse into the forest. Before the Sheriff knew what was happening, they had gone.

It was all so quick. For a time, the Sheriff just stood there and looked. Then at last he saw what had happened. He started to shout at his men: "Go on, after them, you fools. Go on!"

But Robin Hood and Little John were far away by then.

Friar Tuck and the cow

Friar Tuck was a big, fat man, and he loved food. But he did not like the same food every day. He liked a change, and Cook could not always find new things for dinner.

"Must we always eat deer?" Friar Tuck asked. "Are there no other animals a man can eat?"

"You catch them, and I'll cook them," answered the cook. "Bring me a cow, and I'll cut it up for you."

"A good idea," thought Friar Tuck. "But where can I get a cow?"

A few days after that, he was walking back to the forest from Nottingham. It was a hot day, and he stopped at a drinking house. As he sat there, he saw a man leading a cow along the road on a bit of rope. It was a good, fat beast, and Friar Tuck remembered Cook's words. He began to think: "How can I steal this cow and take it back to the forest?"

The man tied the cow to a tree and sat down outside. He called for something to drink. He was a big man, and he did not look friendly. Sometimes he looked up at the cow to see if it was still there. It would be hard to steal it from him.

Friar Tuck steals the cow

Friar Tuck had an idea. He paid for his drink, and
began walking along the road. After a short time,
he stopped and took his shoes off. They were good
shoes. He had just bought them in Nottingham
that day. He put one of them down in the road,
and walked for a little more. He put the other shoe
down in the road. Then he hid in some trees which
were near.

Soon the man with the cow came along the road
and found a shoe. He stopped and looked at it. But
he did not take it. "This is a good shoe," he said
to himself. "But I don't want one shoe without the
other one."

He walked a little more and stopped again.
"What's this?" he said again. "Another shoe. That
makes two." He looked down at his own shoes,
which were old. Then he tied the cow to a tree and
began to walk back along the road. He was going
to get the other shoe.

This was just what Friar Tuck wanted him to do.
As soon as the man had gone, he came out from
his hiding place. Then he untied the cow and led it
away along a side road.

Friar Tuck falls into a river

As he walked along he began to laugh. "A good
day's work," he said to himself. "I've changed two
shoes for one cow." But after he had walked for a

little longer, he did not feel so happy. The stones in the road began to cut his feet. "I was a fool to throw away my shoes," he said. "I don't know how I shall get to the forest like this. I want a horse, not a cow."

Then another idea came to him: "People ride horses. Why don't they ride cows? Why walk when I can ride?"

He got on to the cow's back and gave it a kick. The cow had never had anybody on its back before. Friar Tuck, too, was very fat. It at once became afraid and began to run. It ran and ran all the way to a river. Then it stopped so quickly that Friar Tuck fell into the water.

"You ugly beast," he cried, as he got out of the water. "Look what you've done now." But the cow just put its head down and ate some grass.

Angrily, Friar Tuck tied the cow to a tree again. Then he took his clothes off and laid them on the ground. It was a sunny day. "They'll soon be ready to put on again," he told himself. "I'll have a little sleep in the long grass."

"I like deer best"

As soon as he lay down, he heard somebody coming along the road. He put his head up to see who it was. It was the man who owned the cow! The man looked hot and angry, and Friar Tuck was afraid. "If I put my head down, the man will not see me," he thought.

When he saw the cow the man stopped. "Is this magic, or did I drink too much?" he said. "I tie my cow to one tree, and I find it tied to another." He looked down and saw Friar Tuck's clothes on the grass. "And what's this?" he said. "I find shoes on the road, and now clothes on the grass." He came nearer to get a better look. "But these are too old for anybody," he said, and kicked them into the water. From his hiding place Friar Tuck saw the river take his clothes away.

The man then untied his cow and went off. And Friar Tuck, without shoes or clothes, walked back to the forest. All his friends laughed to see him come back without clothes.

When he had found some other clothes to put on, he went to see the cook.

"What's for dinner?" he asked.

"Deer again," said Cook.

"Good!" said Friar Tuck. "I think I like deer best, after all."

Robin Hood's men came and went as they liked. Some stayed with him for years; others for no more than a few weeks. He did not ask much from them. If they were friendly and fought well with bow and sword, he was happy to have them with him.

His newest man, Randal Wakefield, was very friendly. He laughed all the time, and most of Robin Hood's men liked him. But not all of them did.

"He laughs too much," said Little John. "Sometimes I think he's a little *too* friendly."

"He asks too many questions," said Friar Tuck. "He wants to know too much."

"The forest would be a sad place without men like Randal," said Robin Hood. "I like a man who can laugh when it's cold or raining. He makes the men happy."

"But there's another thing," said Little John. "He has too many friends outside the forest. I've seen him speaking to men from Nottingham. Who knows what he tells them?"

"I don't know what he tells them," said Robin

Hood, "or what they tell him. But it's good for us to talk to people. We may hear things which can help us all – where the Sheriff is; who is making journeys; what is happening in London and York."

Little John said no more. But it was not hard to see what he thought. He thought that Randal Wakefield was a spy!

The rich abbot

One day, not long after this, Randal *did* hear something. A friend told him that a rich abbot was on his way from York to London. He told Robin Hood at once.

Robin Hood was glad to hear this. There had

not been many rich men to steal from in the last few weeks. "This abbot will have a lot of money with him," he said. "We must catch him!"

"We can try," said Little John, "but the forest is big, and there are three roads through it. We can't be everywhere at once. He may have soldiers with him, too. We can't send some men here and some men there. We shall want all our men in one place."

Robin Hood sat down on the ground and began to make marks in the dust with his finger, like this:

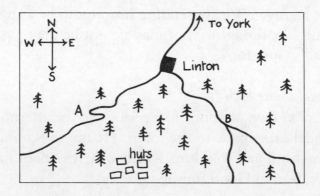

"Look," he said, "this is the road from York. At Linton, the road becomes two roads. The place A is on the road to the west. At the place B, the road to the east becomes two roads. These are the three roads through the forest.

"We can't stop the abbot at Linton. It is out of the forest, and there are too many people there. So the best places are A or B. They are quite near our huts, which are here." He made another mark on the ground. "But we don't know which road he'll take. I'll send a spy to wait at Linton. As soon as the abbot takes one road or the other, our man must come back and tell me. Now who shall I send as our spy?"

"Send me," said Randal, before any of the others could speak.

"Why not?" said Robin Hood. "You were the one who heard about the abbot. You can go."

So Randal went. But again Little John did not look happy. "We are sending him out to be a spy for us," he thought, "but may he not be the Sheriff's spy, too?"

Randal comes back
The next day, at about five o'clock in the afternoon, Randal came back to the forest. He ran to Robin Hood's hut and told him which way the abbot had gone. Robin Hood jumped up.

"Stay here with Friar Tuck," he said. Then, with the others after him, he ran through the trees the way Randal had come. When he was a little way from the huts he led his men towards the east.

Again, Little John was not happy. "Robin," he said, "I don't like it. This Randal may be a spy. We don't know who is waiting for us if we go this way. It could be the Sheriff and his men."

But Robin Hood did not stop. "I know what

I'm doing, Little John," he said. "Look, I can see the road at last."

A fight with the Abbot

The Abbot of St Mary's, York, was not a fat, happy man like Friar Tuck. He had a long, white face and cold, blue eyes. He ate little and thought much – mostly about money. How he loved to put his hands into his moneybags and make the gold run through his fingers! He was thinking about this as he rode through the forest. He was thinking, too, about the Sheriff's letter. A man had brought it to him on the road the day before. "Take the road to the east," the letter had said. "You will meet no thieves on that road."

"How does he know that?" the Abbot asked himself.

Just then, something very big fell out of the tree he was riding under. It hit him so hard that he fell off his horse. All round him other things were falling out of trees and on to his men. He tried to get up, but he could not. Someone was sitting on him! Everywhere men were shouting and the horses were afraid. "What is happening?" the Abbot cried.

Robin Hood's men had hidden in the trees which grew over the road. And when the time came, they had jumped down on to the Abbot and his men. "A-Hood! A-Hood!" they shouted.

It was their fighting cry.

Some of the Abbot's men tried to fight. But most had no time to get their swords out. And those that could soon found Robin Hood's men too good for them. There was a CLASH here, and a DING and a DANG there. But the Abbot's men soon threw their swords down on the ground. Some tried to run away, but there were men in green in front of them on the road, and at their backs.

"Stop, or we shoot!" they cried. And the Abbot's men stopped. Nobody wanted an arrow through his body.

It was all over before they knew it had begun. By the time the Abbot was on his feet again, Robin Hood was taking the moneybags from the Abbot's horse. The Abbot cried out. For him, losing money was like losing an arm or a leg.

The Abbot meets the spy

Some of the men in green stayed with the Abbot's men and horses. The others, with Robin Hood, took the Abbot and his money back to the huts. Friar Tuck and Randal came out to meet them. Friar Tuck rubbed his fat hands when he saw the moneybags. But Randal did not look at all happy.

Robin Hood looked at him. "Randal," he said, "you have done good work."

Then, to the Abbot, he said: "You must meet

our spy. This is Randal Wakefield. He told us you
were coming. We sent him to find out which road
you took. He's our best spy, aren't you, Randal?"

Randal's face became white, and he said nothing.
But the Abbot's face became red and angry. "Is
this the man who has made me lose my gold?"
he thought. "I shall remember his name."

"And now," said Robin Hood to the Abbot,
"you will drink with me. After that you may go
back to your horses and men and start your journey
again."

The Abbot drank. He was afraid not to. He
did not know what he was drinking, but it was
good. "Too good for thieves like these," he
thought. Then Robin Hood and his men took the
Abbot back to the road. By that time it was night.

"We must help the Abbot," said Robin Hood.
"Come here, Randal. You helped the Abbot to
lose his way. Now you can help him to find it
again. You will not want that," he said, taking
Randal's sword from him. "You must not be
afraid of the Abbot and his men. You must now
lead them through the forest." Then he gave the
swords back to the Abbot's men.

"I don't want to go," said Randal. "Without my
sword they may kill me!"

Robin Hood looked at him coldly. "And what
do you think *I* shall do to you if you stay?"

Randal went with the Abbot. The last thing

Robin Hood saw of him was his white face looking back through the night.

The Sheriff's spy

"Why did you do that?" asked Little John when
they had gone. "You sent him off without a sword.
They may do anything to him."

"If they kill him, they will do our work for us.
He was a spy, and tried to kill us all."

"A spy?" said Little John. "I thought so, too,
from the beginning. But didn't he lead us to the
Abbot and his money?"

"No, he did not," answered Robin Hood. "He
told me that the Abbot had taken the other road.
But I knew that the Sheriff was waiting for us on
that road, so I went east. No, Little John, I'm not
a fool. I knew he was a spy from the beginning.
It is sometimes better not to show what we know
too soon.

"Now, open those bags. I want to see how much
the Abbot has paid us for his drink!"

The golden arrow

"No," said the Sheriff. "He'll get away, as he always does."

"But if he comes inside the city gates, how *can* he get away?" asked Baldwin. "And if he doesn't come, we shall still have something to show the Prince. We must find something for him to do, when he stays here."

Baldwin had thought of a new way to catch Robin Hood. This time with an arrow – a golden arrow. Prince John was on his way to Nottingham. And the Sheriff wanted to give him something to look at. Baldwin's idea was a shooting competition. For the man who shot best there would be a golden arrow.

"Robin Hood won't stay in the forest. He won't want another man to win the arrow. He'll come to Nottingham. Then you'll catch him," said Baldwin. "And the Prince will think you are doing good work as a sheriff."

"And what will he think if I *don't* catch him?" asked the Sheriff. "Robin Hood has made fools of us before. I must think about it."

"Don't go, Robin"

The Sheriff did think about it. And as he thought about it, he liked the idea more and more. Soon he began to talk about it as his own idea. But Baldwin did not say anything. The Sheriff always stole his ideas.

The Sheriff sent men out into the country all round Nottingham. They told everybody about the competition. Soon, every man who was good with a bow was talking about it. And before long, this talk came to the ears of Robin Hood and his men.

"Will Robin Hood go to Nottingham, or will he not?" This was the question that everyone asked.

"Robin, don't go," said Maid Marion. "The Sheriff knows your face too well."

"Everybody in Nottingham knows you are the best," said Friar Tuck. "Must you win a golden arrow to show it?"

"I don't like it," said Little John. "I think it's better not to go."

Robin Hood laughed: "And make the people of Nottingham think I'm afraid? No, I shall go. And I shall bring the golden arrow back to the forest."

Prince John is angry

At last, Prince John came to Nottingham. He brought many soldiers with him. Like the Sheriff, he was an angry man. It had been a bad journey

from York and he was angry when he came. But he was even more angry when the Sheriff took him into the forest. There were very few deer that year, and he soon found out why.

"The Prince talks about Robin Hood all the time," said the Sheriff to Baldwin. "If we don't catch him tomorrow, I shall lose my place as sheriff."

Robin Hood is in Nottingham

Next morning, as soon as the city gates opened, people from the country began to come into Nottingham. Many of the men had bows. They all wanted to win the golden arrow. Soon the great open place by the castle was full of people.

At about nine o'clock, one of his men came to see the Sheriff. He had just seen Robin Hood come through the gates.

"Aha!" said the Sheriff, rubbing his hands. "Our fish has bitten. We shall catch him now!"

"Was he alone?" asked Baldwin.

"That man they call Friar Tuck was with him," the man answered. "He looked fatter than he was before."

The Sheriff grew angry. "They all grow fat eating the king's deer. The Prince never stops telling me that. Go back to the gate," he said. "You know what to do when the competition begins."

Robin Hood wins the arrow and runs

In the open place by the castle, the shooting was nearly over. Two men were still shooting. One was one of the Sheriff's men. The other was Robin Hood. Thousands of people stood there looking, but there was no noise. Everybody wanted to see who would win. The Sheriff and Prince John sat on a high place which had been made for them. They, too, could not take their eyes from the shooting.

The things they were shooting at stood by the castle wall. There were black, red, white and blue rings on them, one inside the other. Each bowman was trying to get his arrows in the inner ring.

The Sheriff's man shot three arrows into the inner ring. The Sheriff laughed: "Robin Hood cannot do better than that." The Prince did not answer. His eyes were on Robin Hood.

Robin Hood took up his bow. Nobody made the smallest noise. He, too, shot three arrows. Each arrow hit one of the arrows of the Sheriff's man, so that they fell out on to the ground. Then he took three more arrows and shot them all into the inner ring. They were so near that they were touching.

At once the people began to shout, "Robin Hood! Robin Hood!" The Sheriff looked angry.

"He's won. He must have the arrow," said the Prince.

"He shall have it," said the Sheriff. "But he won't have it for long. The city gates are shut. He won't get out of Nottingham alive."

The Prince stood up and took the golden arrow from the Sheriff. Robin Hood came up and stood in front of him.

"You have won the competition, and I give you this arrow," said the Prince, "but I think you will shoot no more of my deer." He gave a look to the Sheriff, and the Sheriff gave a look to his men. But before they could lay their hands on him, Robin Hood had quickly put the golden arrow in his bow.

"Then I shall shoot a prince," he said. "A golden arrow is too good for any other man." He stood ready to shoot. Nobody moved. Nobody said a word.

At last the Sheriff spoke: "You cannot shoot the brother of your king," he said.

"Then tell your men not to come near me."

"Stand back!" said the Sheriff to his soldiers.

Then everything happened very quickly. Robin Hood jumped down on to the ground. Some of his men were standing with the people of the town. They helped to make a way for him.

He did not run towards the gates. He knew the Sheriff had closed them. He ran to a place by the city walls where Friar Tuck was waiting for him. Friar Tuck had come into Nottingham that

morning with a long rope round his body. It
was that which had made him look fat. Now he
had put the rope over the wall, and Robin Hood
and his men went up and then down it one by one.
It was a good rope. Even Friar Tuck got down
without breaking it!

"Run for your lives," shouted Robin Hood.
And they did. The Sheriff's men were now on
the walls, and arrows began to fall near them.
One hit one of Robin Hood's men, Will Scarlet, in
the leg, and the others had to help him.
, Even then the Sheriff's horsemen were riding
out of the city. The forest was still a long
way, and Robin Hood had a man who could not
walk. "Will the Sheriff's men still catch us after
all this?" he thought.

Saved by Sir Richard

"Put me down and run," said Will Scarlet. "Why
don't you save yourselves? You'll never get to
the forest if you help me."

"I do not throw my men away like old clothes,"
said Robin Hood. "The Sheriff shall not catch
you." He stopped so they could all hear him.
"We are not far from the castle of Sir Richard
at the Lee. Do you remember him? I helped him
when he couldn't pay money to William of Linby.
He may help us now. If we can get as far as his
castle he may take us in."

They walked and ran across some open ground.
The Sheriff's horsemen were not far away. "Go
towards those trees," cried Robin Hood. The
horsemen couldn't get through the trees. "Look!"
shouted Robin Hood. "They must now ride
round." That gave him and his men time to get to
the castle gate.

"Open!" shouted Robin Hood. "Open up or
we die!"

Sir Richard looked out of a window. He ran
down and told his men to open the gate. As soon
as they had got in, the gate was shut again, and
soon after that they heard the Sheriff's horses
outside.

"Open up!" cried someone. It was Baldwin.
"Open up for the Sheriff's men!"

"I open this gate for the king, and for no other
person," Sir Richard answered. "I'm one of the
king's own men, as you know."

"The Sheriff shall hear of this, Sir Richard,"
said Baldwin. "I know you have Robin Hood
there."

"I'll have who I like in my own castle," said
Sir Richard. "Do what you can. I shall not open
my gate."

Robin Hood leads his men out of the castle
Baldwin sent a man back to Nottingham to tell
the Sheriff. The Sheriff sent more men back to

the castle. They stayed there, waiting for Robin
Hood and his men to come out. But they did not
come out. Sir Richard had food for a year, and
he did not open his gates.

The Prince had moved north by this time.
Before he went, he said to the Sheriff: "I'll be
back in Nottingham in September. If you haven't
caught Robin Hood by then, I shall find a new
sheriff. And it'll be bread and water for you. In
a little room under the castle."

The Sheriff was unhappy and afraid. He liked
eating and drinking. "Bread and water will kill
me," he thought. "This time I *must* catch Robin
Hood." So for week after week his men stayed
outside Sir Richard's castle. And still Robin Hood
did not come out.

But Robin Hood was not doing nothing. He
was always looking at the Sheriff's men from the
walls. He saw that they did not always stay awake
at night. So one night, when there was no moon,
he led his men over the castle wall and through
the line of soldiers. Robin Hood's men knew how
to shoot deer in the forest. It was not hard for
them to walk without noise. In an hour, they were
back in the forest again.

Sir Richard is taken
Some weeks after this, a lady and a young boy
rode into the forest. They had come to find Robin

Hood. Soon they met one of his men, who took them to him. Robin Hood was glad to see them. He knew them well. It was the wife and son of Sir Richard at the Lee. The lady had a sad story.

"Oh, Robin Hood!" she cried. "Sir Richard has been taken by the Sheriff! He was out riding, and the Sheriff's men were waiting for him. They caught him and took him to Nottingham. And the Sheriff has taken my castle."

Robin Hood looked sad when he heard this. "It is I who have made all this happen," he said. "But I will find some way to save Sir Richard. Give me a little time to think." He called Little John to him, and they walked off into the forest.

By the time that Sir Richard's wife and son had eaten and drunk, he was back. "There is only one thing to be done," he told them. "I shall send a letter to the Sheriff. By tonight you will be back in your castle, and Sir Richard will be with you again."

"But how can you do all that?" asked the lady.

"Ask no questions, but stay here for the afternoon. Then go to your castle."

Soon after that, Little John went off to Nottingham as quickly as he could.

Robin Hood gives himself to the Sheriff
That evening the lady and her son went back to her castle. The gate was open, and the Sheriff's

men had gone. Sir Richard met her and kissed her. But he did not look happy.

"Is Robin Hood a magician, then?" she asked. "How did he make the Sheriff give you up?"

"He is not a magician," answered Sir Richard sadly, "but a good and brave man. He has given himself to the Sheriff, and the Sheriff has given me back to you."

The Sheriff writes to Prince John

In the forest everybody was sad. Robin Hood had lost the long fight with the Sheriff. There he was, shut up in Nottingham Castle in a little room under the ground with no light. The Sheriff's men stood outside it night and day. This time nobody could save him. He must die.

But when? That was the question. The Sheriff knew that Prince John would come back to Nottingham soon. "Prince John may like to see Robin Hood die," he thought. "I'll write and ask him. Robin Hood will be quite happy to wait a week. He'll have more time to think about it." So he sent a letter to the Prince, who was still in the north, and waited for an answer.

The letter

About ten days after that, a man riding quickly through the forest was stopped by some of Robin Hood's men. At once he became angry. He said

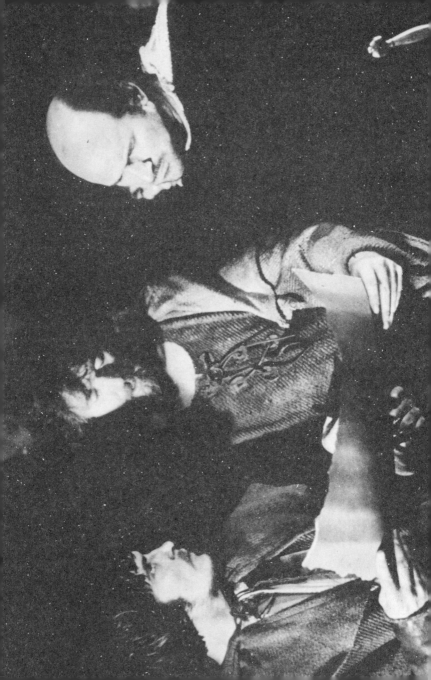

had none. But he did have a letter, and they took him to Little John.

The man then became even angrier. "You cannot stop me," he said. "I have a letter from Prince John to the Sheriff of Nottingham."

"Give me the letter," said Little John. The man did not want to, but he knew he could not say no. "What does this say?" said Little John to Friar Tuck. Little John could not read.

It was a very short letter, and Friar Tuck read it out.

You ASk If you SHOULD WAIT TO kILL ROBIN HOOD. DONT. kILL HIM. HE IS MY FRIEND WHO DOES THIS.

"What can we do?" asked Little John. "We can stop this letter, but that will only save Robin Hood for a time."

Friar Tuck did not answer. He was thinking. He looked at the letter again and again. "Bring me my writing things," he said at last. "I have an idea that may still save him." He sat down at the long table, and made a few small changes to the letter. This is how the letter was now:

You Ask If You Should WAIT TO kILL ROBIN HOOD. DONT kILL HIM. HE IS MY FRIEND. WHO DOES THIS?

Friar Tuck looked round at the faces of Robin Hood's men. "Somebody must take this letter to the Sheriff – somebody the Sheriff doesn't know," he said. "You, Ailred Whitehands. You haven't been with us long. Take this man's horse and put on his clothes—"

"My clothes!" shouted the Prince's man. "The Prince will kill you all for this."

"If he can catch us all," said Little John.

"—and take the letter to the Sheriff," Friar Tuck went on. "Now we've done all we can. Robin Hood must get himself out of Nottingham."

Robin Hood gets back to the forest
The Sheriff did not know what to do. He read the letter again and again. "How can Robin Hood be his friend?" he asked. "What has happened to make him the Prince's friend?"

"He has done many things for the Prince,"

said Ailred. "He is now the Prince's man. The Prince was angry when he heard you had shut him up in your castle."

"Then we must get him out at once," said the Sheriff. "Baldwin, bring him here. Give him new clothes. Give him food and drink."

They brought Robin Hood to the Sheriff. He did not know what was happening. But when he saw Ailred there, he looked a little happier.

"The Prince has work for you, Robin Hood," said Ailred. "He wants you to go back into the forest and save his deer from thieves."

"I would like to stay here with my friend, the Sheriff," said Robin Hood. "I sleep so well on these castle beds. And I haven't had bread and water like his in any other place. But I must do what the Prince says. A horse, please, Sheriff, at once. I have the Prince's work to do."

Soon after that, Ailred and Robin Hood were riding out of Nottingham. Ailred told him all about the letter, and Robin Hood laughed all the way back to the forest.

A new Sheriff of Nottingham?
One week after that, Prince John came back to Nottingham. The Sheriff met him at the gates.

"Well done, man," said the Prince. "Now at last I shall have deer to kill in Sherwood Forest."

"Oh yes," said the Sheriff. "Your friend Robin

Hood is back in the forest and doing your work."

"Back in the forest?" The Prince nearly fell off his horse. "Robin Hood back in the forest? Did he get away?"

"Why, no," said the Sheriff. "I sent him back."

"You did *what*?" shouted the Prince. "Is this a fool I have for a sheriff?" Nobody had ever seen him so angry.

"But your letter..." said the Sheriff, who was now afraid.

"My letter told you to kill him at once, and you have not done so. I will have a new Sheriff of Nottingham!"

The next day, Robin Hood sent the Prince's man back to Nottingham. At last the Prince knew what had happened. But the Sheriff – if we can call him that – stayed shut up. For a week there was no sheriff, as the Prince tried to find a new one. But he soon found that nobody wanted to be sheriff. Nobody wanted to fight with Robin Hood all the time. So at last the old sheriff came back, and the long fight in the forest began again.

List of extra words

abbot *the head man of an abbey, a house of churchmen*

blow a horn

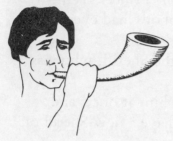

bow and arrows

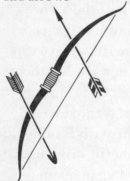

break

castle

competition *when two or more people try to win something*

deer

gate

idea *a new thing that we think about*

laugh *cry "Ha, ha!"*

rope

sail

sheriff *a man who ruled a part of the country for the king*

shoot *send (an arrow) through the air*

spy *a man who goes to see (for his country) what another country is doing*

thief *a person who steals things*

tie

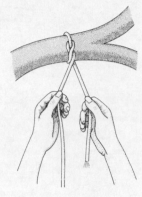